SCIENCE EXPERIMENTS WITH

SIGHT & SOUND

A Division of ABDO
ABDO
Publishing Company

BY ALEX KUSKOWSKI

Consulting Editor, Diane Craig, M.A./Reading Specialist

visit us at www.abdopublishing.com

Published by ABDO Publishing Company, a division of ABDO, P.O. Box 398166, Minneapolis, Minnesota 55439. Copyright © 2014 by Abdo Consulting Group, Inc. International copyrights reserved in all countries. No part of this book may be reproduced in any form without written permission from the publisher. Super SandCastle™ is a trademark and logo of ABDO Publishing Company.

Printed in the United States of America, North Mankato, Minnesota
062013
112013

 PRINTED ON RECYCLED PAPER

Editor: Liz Salzmann
Content Developer: Alex Kuskowski
Cover and Interior Design and Production: Mighty Media, Inc.
Photo Credits: Aaron DeYoe, Shutterstock

The following manufacturers/names appearing in this book are trademarks: Elmer's®, Fiskars®, Sharpie®

Library of Congress Cataloging-in-Publication Data
Kuskowski, Alex.
   Science Experiments with sight & sound / by Alex Kuskowski ; consulting editor, Diane Craig.
      p. cm. -- (More super simple science)
   Audience: 005-010.
   ISBN 978-1-61783-854-5
   1. Optics--Experiments--Juvenile literature. 2. Optical illusions--Experiments--Juvenile literature. 3. Sound--Experiments--Juvenile literature. 4. Science--Methodology--Juvenile literature. I. Craig, Diane. II. Title.
   QC360.K874 2014
   530.078--dc23
                      2012049958

Super SandCastle™ books are created by a team of professional educators, reading specialists, and content developers around five essential components—phonemic awareness, phonics, vocabulary, text comprehension, and fluency—to assist young readers as they develop reading skills and strategies and increase their general knowledge. All books are written, reviewed, and leveled for guided reading, early reading intervention, and Accelerated Reader® programs for use in shared, guided, and independent reading and writing activities to support a balanced approach to literacy instruction.

TO ADULT HELPERS

Learning about science is fun and simple to do. There are just a few things to remember to keep kids safe. Some activities in this book recommend adult supervision. Be sure to review the activities before starting, and be ready to assist your budding scientist when necessary.

KEY SYMBOL

Look for this symbol in this book.

SHARP!
You will be working with a sharp object. Get help!

TABLE OF CONTENTS

SUPER SIMPLE SCIENCE

You can be a scientist! It's super simple. Science is all around you. Learning about the world around you is part of the fun of science. Science is in your house, your backyard, and on the playground.

Find science in paper and markers. Look for science with your eyes and ears. Try the activities in this book. You'll never know where to find science unless you look!

SCIENCE WITH SIGHT & SOUND

Learn about science with sights and sounds. Listen to homemade instruments. Look and find hidden colors. In this book you will see how using your eyes and ears can help you learn about science.

WORK LIKE A SCIENTIST

Scientists have a special way of working. It is a series of steps called the Scientific Method. Follow the steps to work like a scientist.

1 Look at something. What do you see? What does it do?

2 Think of a question about the thing you are watching. What is it like? Why is it like that? How did it get that way?

3 Think of a possible answer to the question.

4 Do a test to find out if you are right. Write down what happened.

5 Think about it. Were you right? Why or why not?

KEEP TRACK

There's another way to be just like a scientist. Scientists make notes about everything they do. So get a notebook. When you do an experiment, write down what happens in each step. It's super simple!

WHAT YOU WILL NEED

aluminum foil

bowl

card stock

cardboard

coffee filter

colored markers

craft sticks

dark blue sheets of paper

drinking glasses

drinking straw

fabric

food coloring

glue

hole punch

paintbrush

paper

paper plate

paper towel tube

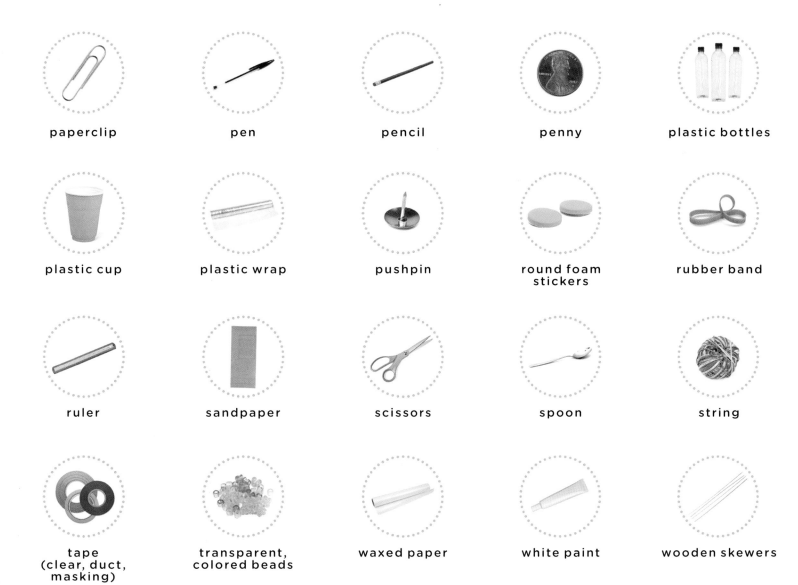

paperclip

pen

pencil

penny

plastic bottles

plastic cup

plastic wrap

pushpin

round foam stickers

rubber band

ruler

sandpaper

scissors

spoon

string

tape (clear, duct, masking)

transparent, colored beads

waxed paper

white paint

wooden skewers

SUPER SPINNING COLOR WHEEL

WHAT YOU WILL NEED

card stock

pencil

ruler

red, blue, and yellow markers

scissors

DIRECTIONS

1. Draw a circle 6 inches (15 cm) across on the card stock. Inside the circle draw a circle 4 inches (10 cm) across. Inside the second circle draw a circle 2 inches (5 cm) across. Draw a line through the center of the circles.

2. On one half, color the inside yellow. Color the middle red. Color the outside blue. On the other half, color the inside blue. Color the middle yellow. Color the outside red.

3. Cut out the circle. Poke a pencil through the center from the back. Hold the pencil between your hands. Move your hands back and forth to spin the circle. Spin it as fast as you can.

WHAT'S GOING ON?

The colors on the wheel **blend** when the wheel spins fast. The colors mix together in your mind. You see colors that are not there.

HAPPY HOMEMADE INSTRUMENT

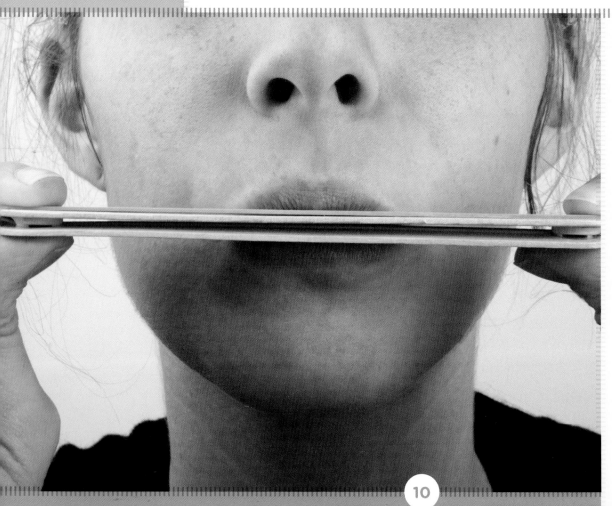

WHAT YOU WILL NEED

2 round foam stickers

2 craft sticks

large rubber band

glue

DIRECTIONS

① Put a foam sticker on each end of a craft stick.

② Put the rubber band around the craft stick over the stickers.

③ Put glue on the rubber band over the foam stickers. Press the other craft stick on top. Press down on it for 1 minute. Let the glue dry.

4   Hold the instrument sideways. Put your lips over it. Blow out so the air goes between the craft sticks.

WHAT'S GOING ON?

Your breath makes the rubber band and the sticks **vibrate**. The vibration makes a sound. You can feel the sticks moving under your lips.

SNEAKY BLIND SPOT SHAPES

WHAT YOU WILL NEED

penny

pencil

paper

ruler

yellow & red markers

DIRECTIONS

1. Trace around the penny on a piece of paper. Move the penny 4 inches (10 cm) away. Trace it again.

2. Draw a star inside the first circle with the yellow marker.

3. Draw a red square in the second circle.

4. Hold the paper in front of you. The star should be on the left. Keep your arms straight. Close your left eye. **Focus** on the star with your right eye. Slowly bring the paper closer.

WHAT'S GOING ON?

Each eye has an **optic nerve** that connects it to the brain. There is a blind spot where the optic nerve enters the eye. As you move the paper closer, the square enters your right eye's blind spot.

SURPRISING COLOR SPLIT

WHAT YOU WILL NEED

coffee filter

ruler

scissors

cardboard

black, green, and brown markers

small bowl

water

DIRECTIONS

1. Cut the filter into a rectangle. It should be 5 inches (12.5 cm) by 6 inches (15 cm).

2. Lay the filter on the cardboard. Draw a thick line on the bottom edge with the black marker. Write the color above it near the top.

3. Repeat with the other markers. Space the lines out evenly.

4. Fill the bowl with water. Dip the bottom edge of the filter in the water. Hold it there for 3 minutes. What happens?

WHAT'S GOING ON?

Colored markers are made up of a mixture of colored inks. When they get wet, the colors separate.

15

FANTASTIC MOVING PICTURES

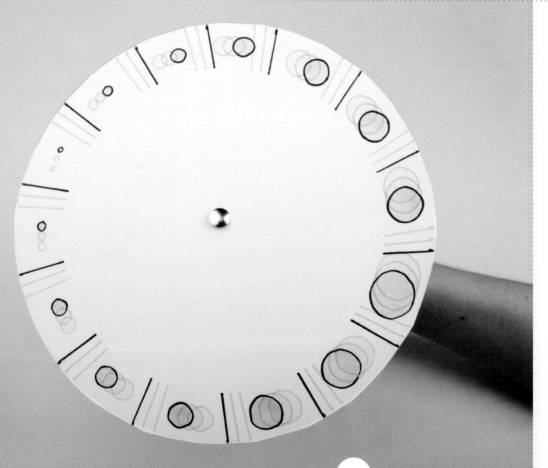

WHAT YOU WILL NEED

paper plate

card stock

pencil

ruler

marker

pushpin

DIRECTIONS

1   Trace around the paper plate on card stock. Cut out the circle.

(2) Make a mark every 2 inches (5 cm) around the edge of the circle. Draw a 1-inch (2.5 cm) line into the circle at each mark.

(3) Draw a picture in each section. Each picture should be almost the same as the one next to it. Just change one thing.

(4) Poke a pushpin through the center of the circle. Push the pin into a pencil eraser. Use the pencil to spin the circle.

WHAT'S GOING ON?

The circle spins too fast for your eyes to see each picture. They blur into each other. It makes the pictures look like they are moving.

LAUGHING FROG NOISEMAKER

WHAT YOU WILL NEED

plastic cup

pen

string, 10 inches (25 cm) long

paperclip

small piece of fabric

water

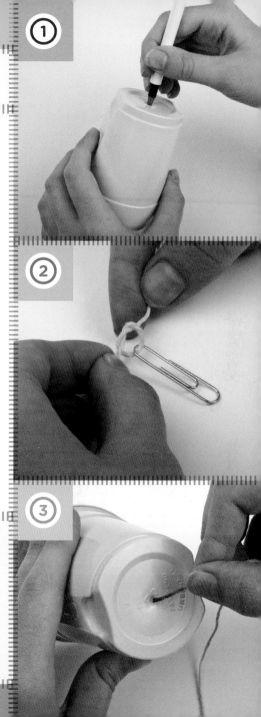

DIRECTIONS

① Use a pen to poke a hole in the bottom of a plastic cup.

② Tie one end of the string to the paperclip.

③ Push the other end of the string into the cup through the hole. Pull it tight. The paperclip should be against the bottom of the cup.

4   Get the fabric wet. Hold the fabric over the string inside the cup. Pull so the fabric slides along the string. Do you hear a frog?

WHAT'S GOING ON?

The noise is made by the fabric rubbing against the string. The sound **bounces** off the sides of the cup. This makes the sound louder.

19

SOUNDS INSIDE YOUR HEAD

WHAT YOU WILL NEED

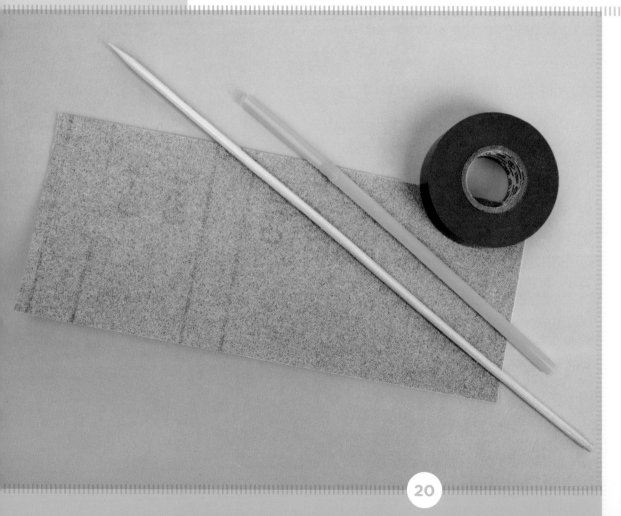

wooden skewer

drinking straw

tape

sandpaper

DIRECTIONS

1. Put the skewer through the straw. One end of the straw should be even with the flat end of the skewer.

2. Put tape around the other end of the straw. Tape it to the skewer.

3. Hold the straw between your teeth. Plug your ears with your fingers.

4. Drag the point of the skewer across the sandpaper. What do you hear?

WHAT'S GOING ON?

Dragging the skewer across the sandpaper makes sound waves. The **vibrations** from the sound waves go up the skewer. They pass through the bones in your head. That lets you hear the sound!

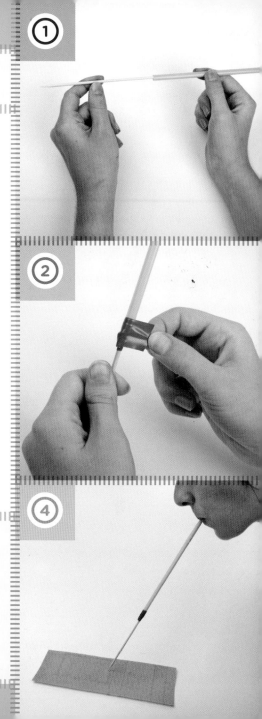

OUT-OF-SIGHT SPACESHIP

WHAT YOU WILL NEED

2 dark blue sheets of paper

paintbrush

white paint

tape

plastic wrap

DIRECTIONS

1. Paint white dots all over both sheets of paper. Paint them in a **random** pattern. Let the paint dry.

2. Cut a spaceship out of one sheet of paper. Cut a strip of paper for a handle. Tape the end of the strip to the spaceship.

3. Place the second sheet on a flat surface. Cover it with plastic wrap. Tape two sides of the plastic wrap to the table.

4. Slide the spaceship under the plastic wrap. Can you see it? Use the handle to move the spaceship back and forth. What changes?

WHAT'S GOING ON?

The spaceship **blends** in with the background when it's still. It is easier to see when it moves. You have special brain cells that help you see movement.

MYSTERIOUS MIRROR IMAGES

WHAT YOU WILL NEED

clear packing tape

ruler

scissors

paper towel tube

marker

card stock

hole punch

tape

aluminum foil

glue

transparent, colored beads

waxed paper

rubber band

DIRECTIONS PART 1

1. Cut two pieces of packing tape 2 inches (5 cm) long. Press the sticky sides together. Trace one end of the tube on the tape. Cut out the circle.

2. Trace one end of the tube on the card stock. Cut out the circle.

3. Punch a hole in the center of the card stock circle.

4. Tape the card stock circle to one end of the tube.

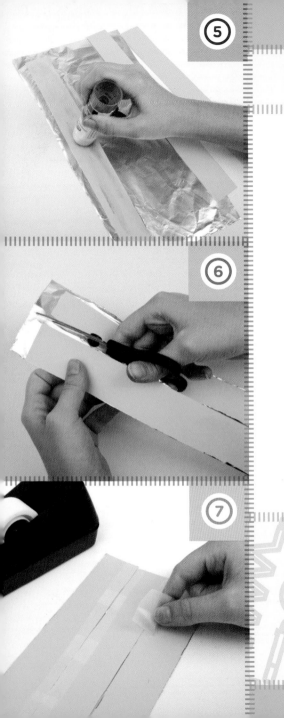

DIRECTIONS PART 2

⑤ Cut three strips of card stock. They should be 10½ inches (26.5 cm) by 1⅜ inches (3.5 cm). Tear off a piece of aluminum foil. Glue the card stock strips to the dull side of the foil. Smooth out the foil.

⑥ Cut the foil around the card stock strips.

⑦ Lay the strips foil side down with the long edges touching. Tape along the long edges.

DIRECTIONS PART 3

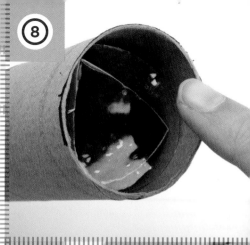

(8) Fold the strips into a triangle-shaped tube. The foil should face in. Tape the edges. Put the triangle inside the paper towel tube. Put the tape circle in the tube. Push it in until it's against the end of the triangle tube.

(9) Fill the end of the tube with beads.

(10) Cover the end with waxed paper. Wrap a rubber band around it to hold it on.

11 Look through the hole. Point the tube at a light. Turn the tube as you look through it.

WHAT'S GOING ON?

The light shines through the beads. As the tube turns, the pattern changes. Each foil strip reflects the light. It also reflects the other foil strips. A kaleidoscope is a way to see endlessly reflected patterns.

COLORFUL WATER VIBRATIONS

WHAT YOU WILL NEED

4 drinking glasses

water

food coloring

spoon

DIRECTIONS

1   Put a different amount of water in each glass.

②   Put a different color of food coloring in each glass of water.

③   Tap the side of each glass with a spoon. The glasses will make different sounds.

④   Put the glasses in order from highest to lowest.

WHAT'S GOING ON?

Tapping a glass causes the water and glass to **vibrate**. The vibrations make a sound. The amount of water affects the size of the vibrations. This affects how high the sound is.

RECYCLED PLASTIC PANPIPE

WHAT YOU WILL NEED

3 plastic bottles

water

duct tape

This panpipe will have you dancing!

DIRECTIONS

① Put a different amount of water in each bottle.

② Put the bottles in a line. Make sure they are touching. Tape the bottles together around the middle.

③ Hold the bottles with both hands. Purse your lips and blow across the top of each bottle. Can you hear a difference?

WHAT'S GOING ON?

When you blow across the top of a bottle, the bottle **vibrates**. The vibrations make a sound. The amount of water in the bottle affects how high the sound is.

CONCLUSION

You just found out that science can be super simple! And you did it using sight and sound. Keep your thinking cap on! What other experiments can you do with sight and sound?

GLOSSARY

blend – to match the surrounding environment.

bounce – to spring up or back after hitting something.

focus – to concentrate on or pay particular attention to.

nerve – one of the threads in the body that take messages to and from the brain.

optic – having to do with the eye or vision.

random – without any order, purpose, or method.

vibrate – to make very small, quick movements back and forth.